The Great Physician

Medicinal Poetry for the Anthropocene

The Great Physician
Medicinal Poetry for the Anthropocene

Stephanie Mines, PhD

KINDRED WORLD
PUBLISHING HOUSE

© 2024 DOM Project

All rights reserved. This book, or parts thereof, may not be reproduced in any form without permission, except in the case of brief quotations embodied in critical articles and reviews.

Book and cover design by Richard Stodart

Photos provided by the author

"How to Write a Poem in a Time of War", from AN AMERICAN SUNRISE: POEMS by Joy Harjo. Copyright © 2019 by Joy Harjo. Used by permission of W. W. Norton & Company, Inc.

Kindred World
P.O. Box 3653
Williamsburg, Virginia 23187

hello@kindredmedia.org
www.kindredworld.org

ISBN: 978-1-7366517-1-1

Library of Congress Control Number: 2023941649

Printed in the USA

To the children of the future.

The art of medicine has its roots in the heart.
  — PARACELSUS

We have to melt the ice in the heart of humanity.
  — UNCLE ANGAANGAQ ANGAKKORSUAQ

How to Write a Poem in a Time of War

Someone has to make it out alive, sang a grandfather to his grandson,
His granddaughter, as he blew his most powerful song into the hearts of the children,
There it would be hidden from the soldiers,
Who would take them miles, rivers, mountains from the navel cord place
Of their origin story.
He knew one day, far day, the grandchildren would return, generations later
Over slick highways constructed over old trails,
Through walls of laws meant to hamper or destroy, over the libraries of
The ancestors in the winds, born in stones.
His song brings us to his home place in these smoky hills.
Begin here.

  — JOY HARJO

Table of Contents

Introduction *9*
The Anthropocene *11*

ANCESTORS *13*

Justice *15*
The Bridge *17*
The Girl Who Split Herself Apart: A Fable *18*
The Parts *19*
The Seer *20*
The Baptism *24*
1933 *25*
The Nameless Lost *28*
Homage to Meridel LeSueur *30*
Alchemical Dream *32*
Born Again *34*
The Revolution Is in the Voices of Women *37*
What Can I Offer the Children of Ukraine? *38*
The Mother Trees Admonish Mr. Putin *40*
Titration *42*
I Am the Crone of Endless Tears *44*

THE ELEMENTS *47*

Earth Elements Rendezvous *49*
The Wood Element Speaks *50*
The Art of Differentiation: For the Air Element *52*
Sequoia: Wood Element Keening *53*
Glare: Glacial Melt *56*
Making Fire from Bone *57*
I Was Born as Creative Fire *58*

Healing   59

The Great Physician   61
Who Are You?   62
American Waiting Room   64
The Black Madonna   66
Beyond Traumatic Repetition   67
The Texture of Oppression   68
Trauma, You Have Schooled Me   70

The Evolution of Consciousness   73

The Line   75
The Embryo, Climate Crisis, and the Pandemic   76
My Crone Years   77
Raw   78
Grandmother at the End of Time   79
Balance   80
Mother   82
After   84
The Earth Inhabits My Mind   86

The Human Family   87

Eldering   89
Raw #2   90
Broadcast from a Nation in Mourning   92
No Waiting   94
Creativity Rising   95

True Embodiment   97

Before I Die   98
The Distance of the Night   100
I Am the Violinist in the Bomb Shelter   103
We Are the Messenger Birds   104
In the Time of Massacres, My Grandmothers Awaken Me   106

The Great Turning   109
About the Author   111

Introduction

The invitation I received from Lisa Reagan at Kindred World Publishing House to assemble a collection of my poems as a chronicle of these times stopped me in my tracks. It led me to an internal retrospective of my life in which I saw that I was born to be a poet as well as a healing artist. Though I had inhabited the world of the writer fully, whole-heartedly, and with great passion when I lived in San Francisco during the 1970's and 1980's, I nevertheless was drawn out of it. Forces I would never have predicted magnetized me into the realms of healing and healthcare and then to climate activism. These pulls seemed to be products of the times that I surely chose to inhabit. Or did they choose me? It is difficult to discern.

Making art is liberating, and, in the liberation, there is always joy. Yet, my poems are drenched with grief. There is no escaping it. Grief is everywhere, and increasingly so, as we seem bent on self-destruction, annihilating species, and violence against children.

I should be accustomed to it. My life has been marked by irrevocable losses. This is underscored by the crushing impact of the Anthropocene. The loss that is the most brutal, the most devastating, is the loss of our children's future. I am speaking of the children of the world, born and unborn, as well as my own children and grandchildren.

I speak as a woman who lost her childhood to abuse and violence. I am someone who experienced the absence of an anchoring, stable adult to mitigate the horror around her. Aside from the occasional presence of my grandfather, who died before I reached adolescence, I was abandoned by the adults in my world. My father returned from war forever broken, and my mother could not withstand nor offset his attacks. I cannot separate the abuse of the earth from the abuse and violence inflicted on me and increasingly on children and youth today. My own formative experiences of not being accompanied, not being honored and respected, not being seen or heard, feels like it bonds me to our living earth.

By failing to protect, regenerate, treasure, and honor the natural world as our most precious gift and sanctuary, we have abandoned our children.

What is a poet to do in the face of this aberration? In the aching of my grief, I offer these articulations as a form of action from my heart. As someone who trained to be a therapist, I know that healing often happens through mirroring. If these poems are mirrors for your felt experience and are therefore healing, I will have fulfilled one aspect of my destiny.

Stephanie Mines, PhD

The Anthropocene

The word Anthropocene combines the root "anthropo," meaning "human," with the root "-cene," which is the standard suffix for "epoch."

The Anthropocene defines Earth's most recent geologic time period as being human influenced or anthropogenic. This is based on overwhelming global evidence that atmospheric, geologic, hydrologic, biospheric and other earth system processes are now being altered by humans.

The Anthropocene is distinguished as a new period either after or within the Holocene, the current epoch, which began approximately 10,000 years ago (about 8000 BC), with the end of the last glacial period.

Source: *The Encyclopedia of the Earth*

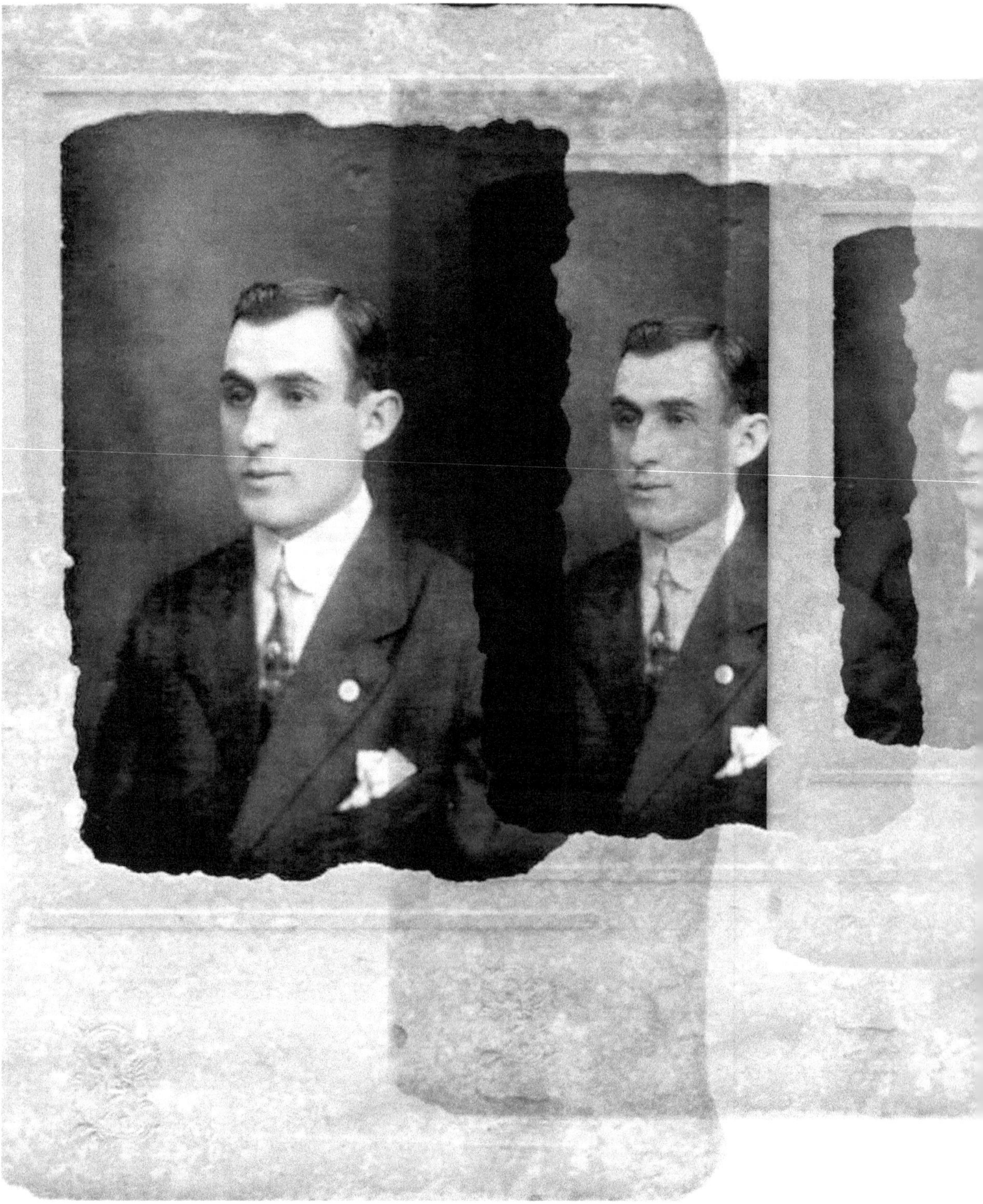

ANCESTORS

It was not until I moved to the Pacific Northwest that I actually understood the language of the Mother Trees. Then, I began to think of my ancestors in a different light. Because my family dynamics were so strained, it has been a journey for me to find the resources that are in my lineage. The Mother Trees taught me how to do that.

I was a lone wolf in my family because I could never match the expectations of Jewish womanhood that were presented to me. My passions for writing, literature, poetry, jazz, and leftwing political activism, never resembled anything like the homemaking and marriage expected of me.

Add to that the violence, the raging, the sexual abuse, and near-criminal behavior of my family members, all of which were supposed to remain secret, and you have a very unseemly lineage, one no one wants to claim.

But in the rich old-growth forest of the Pacific Northwest I discovered the true meaning of ancestry in the entangled root systems under my feet. They were my pathway and my challenge, frequently tripping me up and landing me injured, scared and flat on my face. Have you ever tried walking on an ancient old-growth forest floor? Your eyes have to be glued to your feet as any wayward glance means your shoe will catch on one of the thousands of roots that has erupted upward. The Mother Trees are always trying to reach out to us.

Face planting on the forest floor can be a shamanic experience. Breasts smashed on moss, wrinkles etched in mud, the granular, wet, black earth making body-sculpture of you, you are met with the intimacy you have always longed to experience. The ceaseless parade of rain that is the Pacific Northwest merges with the sweat of your body and ego dissolves into the mess that you become. No drugs needed for shamanic awakening here.

The poems that follow mingle all my disparate ancestries. I come from

Eastern Europe, Belarus, and the constantly shifting borders of Russia, Poland, and Ukraine—places where war is raging right now as I compile these poems.

I come from the Bronx, New York, as well as Asia. I come from the Pacific Northwest, Eire, and other lands I would never have guessed were in my blood—lands like Mexico and Norway—places that did not seem related to me until I fell onto the body of our living earth. She is my ancestry.com.

Justice

My grandmother's voice was coated with the mucosa of grief.
She mired us in the soundscape of all that disappeared.
My grandfather cloaked himself in outsized silence,
The invisible witness cultivating awareness,
Until he was blown away like dust,
Taking with him the secret of his peace.
I call him forward now out of the mists of silent men
Who knew but could not speak,
Who watched and then retreated.
The time has come now for you, Grandpa,
The tailor who can mend the torn fabric of the tribe.
Say it now, and end the repetition,
Say it for all the children blinded by hopelessness,
Grandpa. Tell them of the redemption.
Tell them about our love for one another,
The secret you sent me with your eyes
As you drank tea by the old samovar,
The only remnant left, and gave me the sugar cube,
Steeped in the dark blend of
Our enduring vitality.

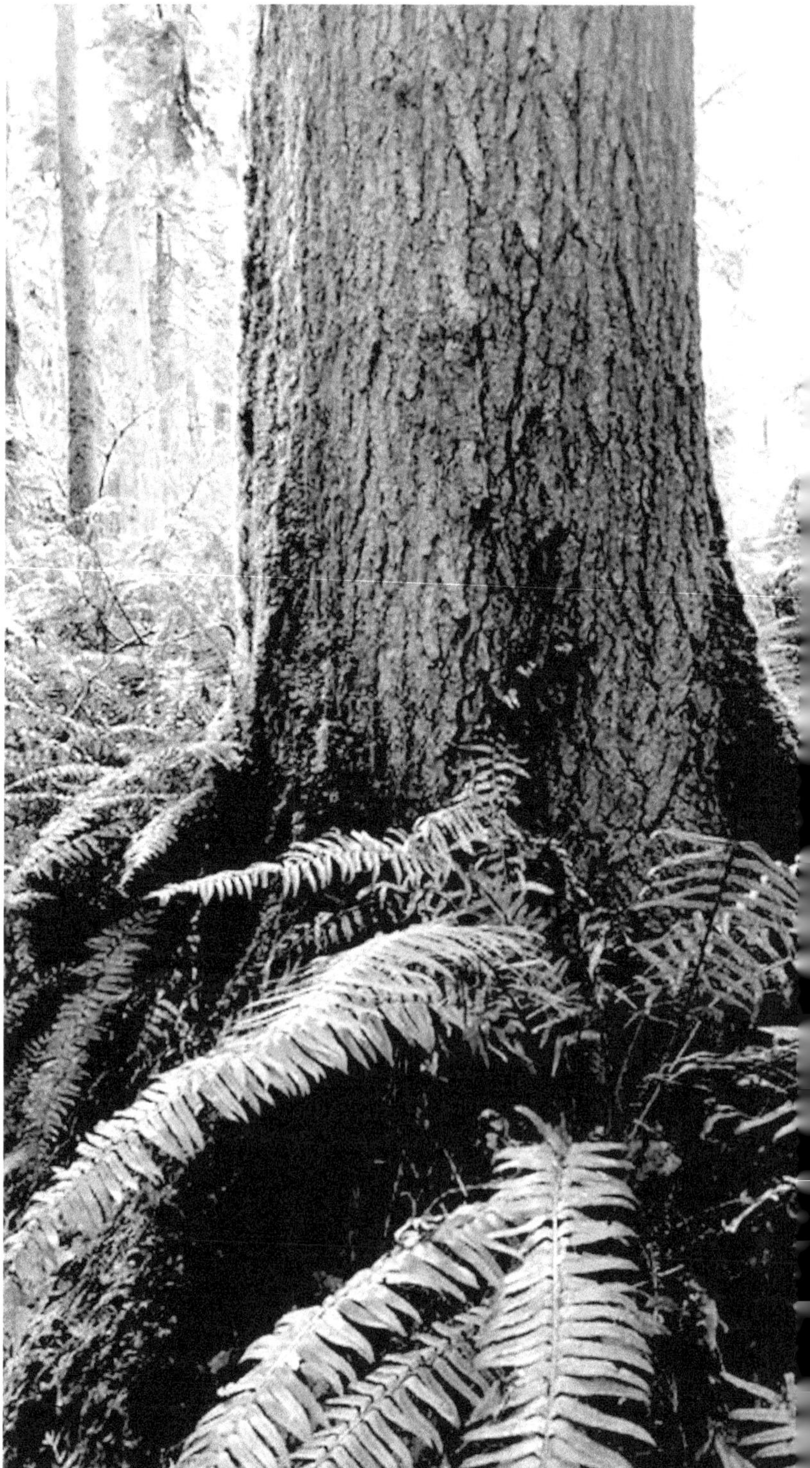

The Bridge

I have become more porous with these waves of awakening.
The shields are remaking themselves
In the interval between now and the birth of the new humanity.
I must act as a bridge, the Mother Trees tell me,
Whenever I can meet with them in solitude.
They comfort me by saying that this is not the only time.
"There is an endlessness in this earth," they say,
"And you are part of the endlessness."
They tell me that just as I feel the danger and the pain,
So can I know their eternity.
"You will always be a child," they say to me,
"Though your skin has become lined as parchment,
And your hands roped by the purple blood of your family's long-lost Royalty.
You remain to us but a beginning spark of the embryonic intelligence
That ignites the flame of all life."
They tell me that all the children that have been lost are returning now,
Reborn in the ocean of love.
They carry the redeeming spirit that will deliver the leaders we are.
"This world is aching for the return of original brilliance," they say,
"The return of our sanity."
"Speak," they say to me, the Mother Trees,
Draped in robes of velvet moss, alight with the jewels of the sun.
"Speak from the place where you are one of us."

The Girl Who Split Herself Apart
A Fable

Once there was a girl conceived by Rage and Fear.
As she found form there was screaming, blood,
Terror and thrashing violence.
The girl was broken and beaten even before she
Emerged from the body of her mother, Fear.
She hid from her father, Rage, and cried ceaselessly.
Unable to bear her parents' world of relentless conflict
Where she was imprisoned, the girl split herself apart.

She used her breath.

She blew herself apart until she had no breath left.

From the force of her passion to live she mobilized

The breath that ripped her asunder.

One self was on the outside, and visible;

The others hidden in the folds of her flesh.

The Parts

The outside part was the Good Daughter.
She was dutiful and obedient.
Another was the Exiled One,
Enraged; rebellious.
The Good Daughter erased the Exiled One,
Except at night when she glimpsed her
Just before sleep
Through half-closed eyes,
Lurking like a stalker.

Born of struggle,
Nursed by struggle,
Kin to struggle,
Struggle that is hidden,
Struggle that is silent,
Struggle masked by duty.

This was her split apart life
Another prison but of her own making.

The Exiled One entangled her limbs within the
Folds of the flesh and organs of the girl.
She twisted and turned
Until the girl noticed her
As discomfort.
Who are you?
The girl asked.
Why are you hurting me?

The Seer

The Exiled One had a secret friend called
The Seer
Who was her voice.
When the girl asked about the pain
The Seer answered for the Exile.
"I am the purpose for which you came."

The girl was confused
And sought comfort for the pain
Elsewhere.
Repeatedly.

Then, something happened in the world where the girl lived.
It became dark with despair.
The darkness surrounded every tree, every forest, every growing thing.
It covered city and countryside;
It shrouded oceans, rivers and lakes;
It silenced the birds;
It enveloped rich and poor alike,
Young and old.

It was so dark that the people were locked in place,
As if blinded by the dark.
Even the most beautiful, the most vibrant
Were cloaked in despair and darkness.
There were no leaders; no one brought a light.

The Exiled One was accustomed to darkness

And restrictions.

Buried, entangled, interwoven

With the very cells of the girl

Her own voice was muffled.

Her only way of speaking was through

Pain and the words of her friend, the Seer.

The Seer, knowing she was enlisted for this time,

Declared the

Separated parts,

Scattered, luminous

Embers glowing in the dark night of the world,

Longing to be reunited into one flame.

The Seer knew

This was the moment.

The Seer turned to the Exiled One

In her masked radiance.

She saw that the Exiled One was

Alight with the fire of hope;

A fire that she had kindled

All these years of exile.

And in seeing that light

The Seer collected and sorted the Exile's buried words

And whispered them to the girl.

"Here in the bowels of your being

Is she who knows how to find her way in

The mystery.

This is the cycle of reunification, long awaited,

Hard won.

Listen to the Exile.

Your rebel within,

Your Ally.
Exiled by
Mother Fear
Remember?
Claim wholeness now
For we are one."

The Good Daughter heard this as her own thought
And reflected.
She sat in the swirling darkness of the time
That forbid her distractions,
The avoidance at which she was skilled,
And remembered
How she blew herself apart
Long ago.
She winced, re-experiencing the pain,
And her father Rage
Reappeared to face her, he who she had long
Sequestered.
But at the same instant
She, who was no longer The Girl but The Woman,
Realized that the pain and Rage were signals,
Merely memories,
And her heart ached
For the courageous beauty she had exiled.

She cried in her loneliness
And her arms stretched out
Before her
In the gesture of her
Longing.

The Seer recognized this as The Sign

And spoke

In her own tongue,

The Woman Voice.

"I was here before Rage and Fear

Conceived you," said the Seer.

"I know unity and I bring our parts

Home.

Good Daughter, Exile and

Seer

Live together

In this

Precious body

You have saved.

This body is Our

Vessel; Our

Vehicle of speech and action,

Embracer and boundary maker,

Artist and strategist,

Nurturer and leader.

Woman you are Daughter of the Earth,

Born of your own

Intention;

Global Citizen of the World;

Warrior for

Peace and Justice;

This is your time."

The Baptism

Written 2/3/06
Oklahoma City
Following a Cranial Session with Physical Therapists Micha Sale,
Margo Hayes, and Kay Davis

I am with you now.
I have filled your cranial bones and sutures with light.
I have imbued your intelligence with Love.
I have softened your frontal lobe and widened your parietal lobes.
I have molded your tears into a balm for your sphenoid.

I have entered you with Light.
The wounds of rude entries have been eradicated and your tissue
Soldered with the burning torch of My Presence.

I have entered you with Consciousness,
Knowing full well who you are and who I Am.

This is the baptism you have invoked through prayer.
I have heard your cries and I have answered and you hear me.
Let me fill your vision with mine
And all that you desire will be yours.

1933

Sedie, Lona, Faye, Pearl
Minnie, Julie, Rose
Lined up, zafusen,
Head to toe
In the narrow beds.
Grandpa staying up to
Put bricks, hot from the stove,
That he wrapped in rags,
Into each bed, under each pair of small feet,
So the heat could rise.
"As you go from Zarasofel on your way to Zinfarofel,
Just you go a little further on;
There's a little railroad depot known quite well by all the people
Called Jan Quoach Jan Jan Jan;
Hey Jan Hey Jan Quoach Hey Jan Vili Hey Jan Quoach,
Hey Jan Quach Jan Jan Jan."
Bube singing, her voice quaking in the old way
That was called beautiful,
The words cracking like egg shells,
No music,
Just the plaintive song of going forward,
The white puffs of her voice visible in the
Black frozen air of
The Bronx apartment,
Behind the failing candy store.

1933 is the year Faye became known as
Fligalach, little wing,
Because she was so thin she was brittle
Like the wishbone
From the chicken Bube cooked,
Leaving the feathers she plucked
In a pile to stuff pillows,
Saving the bones and the guts
For the soup that
They all tasted
In their dreams.

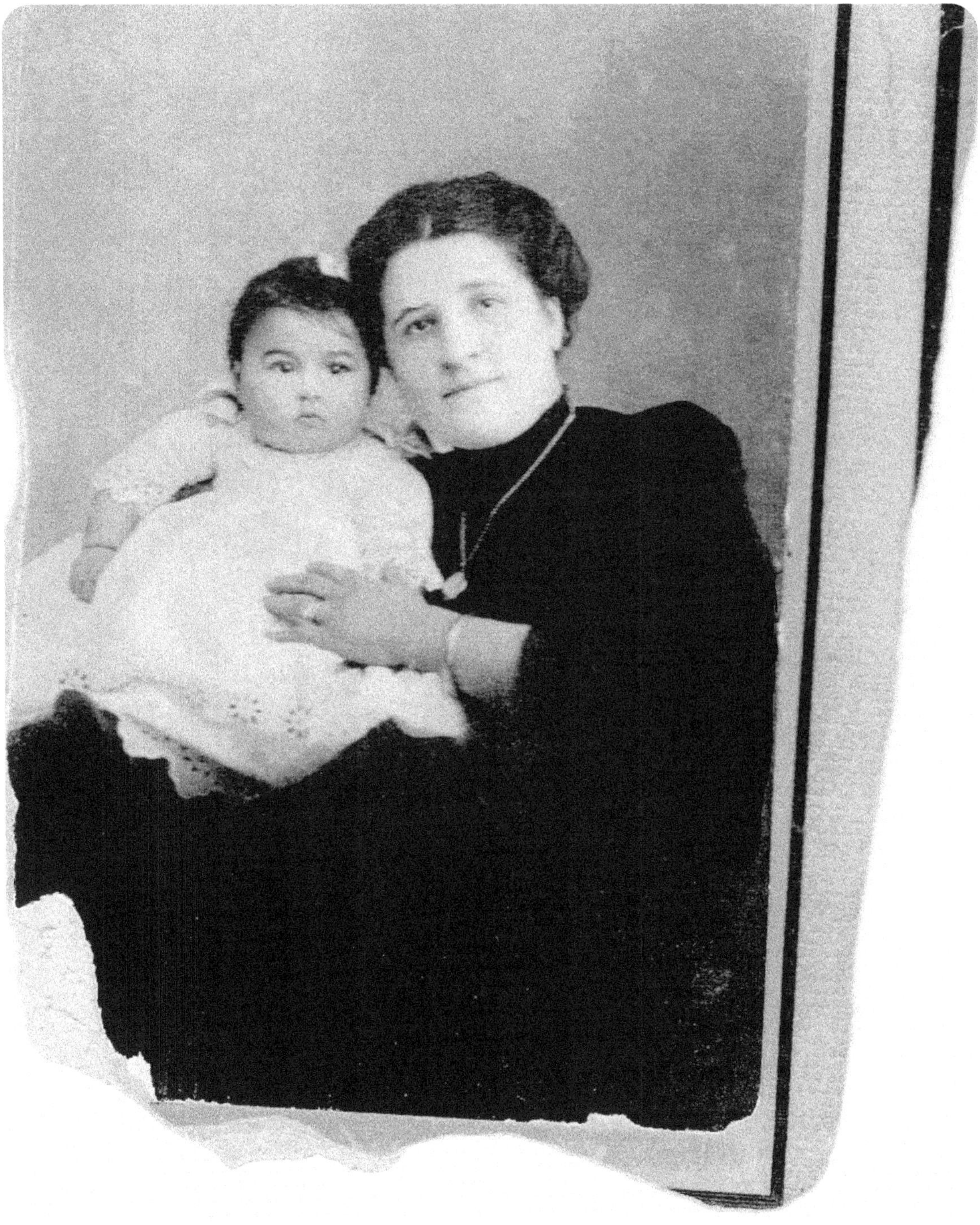

The Nameless Lost

In their rush to evacuate
Each time their lands were seized
And their lives threatened,
My people left behind
All treasure,
Except that the ash of the forgotten
Is sequestered in my lung tissue.
Bits of porcelain and wax are there too,
And the crushed fragrance of relatives and
Friends who spoke of my line
With love. Nameless and lost:
The stories and the roots,
The assurance of place and connection,
Except that the ash of the forgotten
Is sequestered in my lung tissue.
I carry it everywhere.
It is the wheeze in my breath,
The rattle on the inhale at night
To awaken the untold
That I have always known.
Who was the first to eschew
The sacred sharing of pain?
That liar haunts us. I will
Evaporate the myth of false protection.
It is poisonous and antidotes resilience.

I walk in the threadbare shoes of immigrants.

The hungry, invisible tribes that swallowed my teachers are gone,

So that I must search in every cell

For the winding rope of the serpent

That unfolds through my throat

With the wisdom to draw back the

Curtain of illusion, to diffuse the vapor of deceit, and

Illuminate the translucent truth

That is ready to rise

From my pelvic floor,

The springboard of

Homecoming.

Homage to Meridel LeSueur
On the Anniversary of Her Death: 11/13/96

You held my hand
As no one ever has before or since;
Looking in my eyes
With your piercing gaze
You named me
Persephone.
You stepped out of the darkness today
To rally your daughters;
My heart is blessed with tears
To be amongst them.
How did I find you then
And how did I find you again today
On the anniversary of your death?
How did I know?
It was you,
O my ancestor,
O Woman of Valor,
You called me again.
I am humbled, humbled,
On my knees,
Head to the ground.
I am humbled.
Is it because today marks the end of hope

And the beginning of truth?
Is it because today the call of the groundswell
Echoes through the skies?
Is it because you know what it means to be silenced
And to reclaim your voice?
And so you rally your daughters now
And sing lullabies to
All the children of all times.
O my beloved mother,
You come forward today
To hold me fast to my path.
You are the Healer Warrior,
You are the Writer Activist,
You are the Mother Leader,
You are the the one who was silenced
And reclaimed her voice.
O my beloved mother
You come forward today
To hold me fast to my path.

Alchemical Dream

O my ancestors,
Give me the elixir of your love.
I search for it
In the embryology of my dreams.
I rise from your dark mineral waters
Singing jazz,
Moving in ways you have never seen.
I am loud and voluptuous.
I cannot be contained.
I am raucous.
I speak out of turn.
I break the rules.
I am the sperm and the egg.
I demolish the haunting with my poems.
You who were shuttered in the secrecy of pain,
Stripped of your wisdom,
Masquerading as white goyim.
I reveal you from where you were
Hidden from your own sight.
O my ancestors,
Give me the elixir of your love.
Let us drink it together,
Sit down to a meal,
Sleep in the same room,
Wake to the sight of our
Bright eyes delirious with reunion.
O my ancestors,
Bless me with your atonal incantations.

Liberate all the beautifully naughty children,
Like me,
Into our genius.
Let us clap our hands and shout,
Breathe in the pine scented air of our mountains,
Swim in the cool frothy waters of the
Rivers of Splendor
That regenerates our cells.

Born Again

We unfold downward,
Towards the Earth,
Crying like babies
Who were uprooted and then
Forced fed into growth
Without ever blooming.
Top heavy
We are crippled on stalks
Intended to connect us
Above and below
But without the strength to do so
Having never been taught alignment.
We adapt
Into curvatures
Desperate for gravitas,
Agonizingly seeking sun,
Restlessly re-configuring
This way and that,
Disoriented,
Following whatever draws us
Back
To the ground.
Finally, the voice of
Gravity wins.

It humbles our wayward flowering,
Invites the unpretentious and unremarkable.
Gravity pulls us down into Earth's belly
Where we can sleep for a while,
Sobbing, "Mama Mama,"
Sucking on the juices,
Eating the dirt,
Ravenous,
Thirsty,
Until
We
Ri
Se
Up.

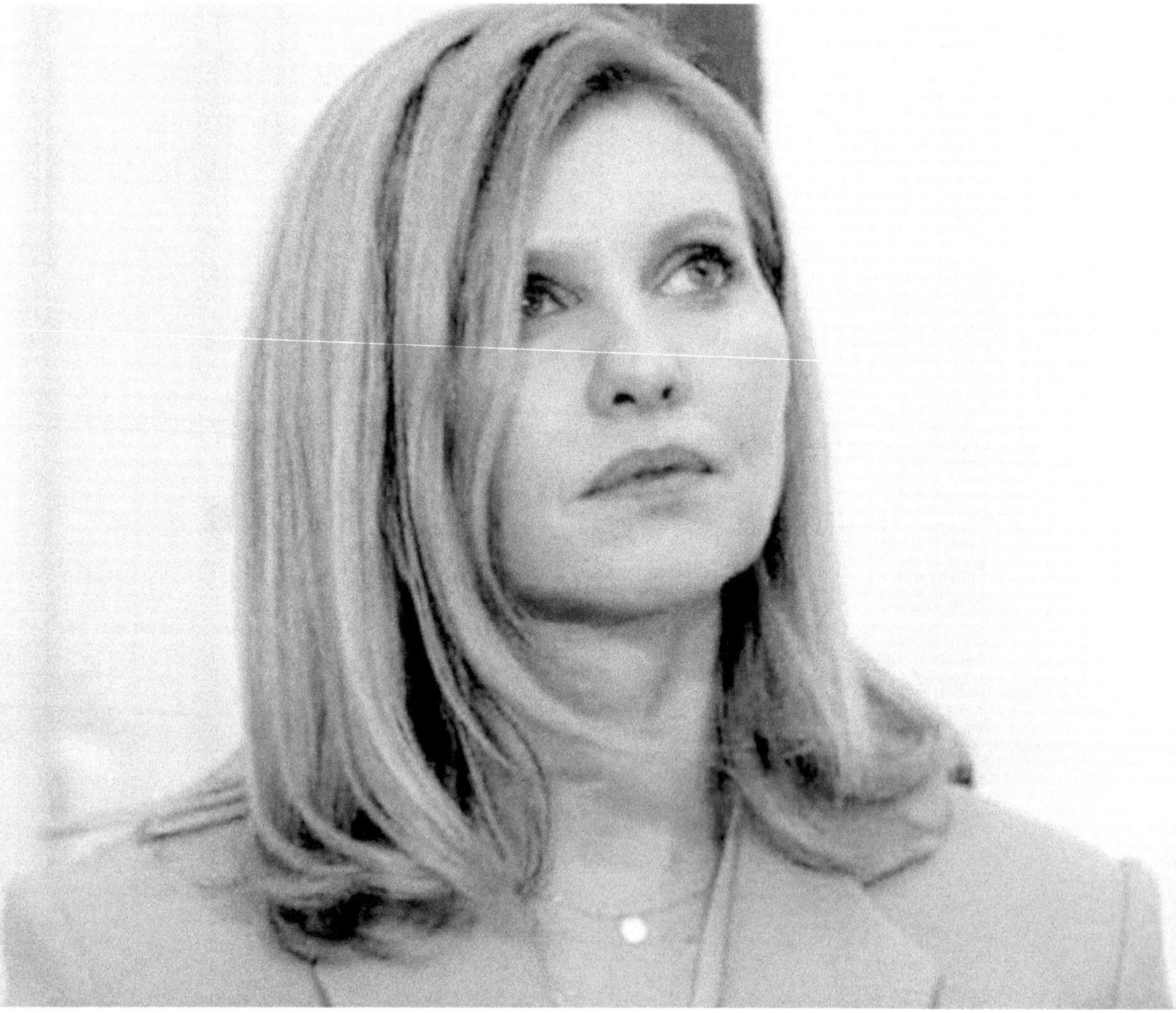

The Revolution Is in the Voices of Women
International Women's Day 2022

Dedicated to Olena Zelenska

The revolution is in the voices of women
Who speak to everyone in the room,
Tuned to the rhythms of the Earth.
The revolution is in the voices of women
Who are not waiting for anyone or anything else.
We are the weavers of merciful compassion and authentic outrage.
We make the future into now.
Our bodies are the economics of the new world.
We are ancient and innovative
Devising economics that leave no bowls empty.
That was always the design.
The revolution is in the voices of women who know that
Visions, dreams, planning, implementation, manifestation
Are one and the same gesture of simplicity
From the unified field of being.
The revolution is in the voices of women
Who have moved beyond trauma to wholeness.
If you can hear us, then
It is done.

What Can I Offer the Children of Ukraine?

Tonight, I ask myself,
What can I offer the children of Ukraine,
Those who are born and those who are yet unborn?
My grandmother's heart,
Already trampled and in disarray,
Bleeds; the tender outer skin broken to
Merge my suffering with theirs.
I am impotent and so far from you, little ones,
Just as I am far from my own grandchildren,
All I can manage
Are prayers for the soldiers of Russia to stop.
Asking that they do not obey orders of destruction
That kills the lives that are our future.
I ask them to awaken to how
Each death is their own.
My granddaughters roll their eyes
When I name the children of Ukraine as kin.
They look away in disdain
When I speak of a universal genealogy,
And how we, they and I, carry
The embryology of all time in our bones.
My pelvis aches when I look into the emptying well
Of humanity's destiny.
I am a carrier of the legacy of the feminine,
And my voice is eschewed, even in my own home.

Still, I ask myself tonight,
What can I offer the children of Ukraine,
Those born and those yet unborn?
My own arms are theirs,
Guiding them to self-embrace,
To hold themselves dear in every moment,
Precious lights that will never dim.

The Mother Trees Admonish Mr. Putin

In the shushing moss cushioned
Sheltering embrace of the Mother Trees,
Whose comfort I seek for my agonized tears of helplessness,
I hear the Mothers admonishing Mr. Putin.
"No, no, no," they hum,
"You, Mr. Putin, do not shape the future. Not now or ever."
I look up, glancing at each of them, regally draped and dappled.
The tallest one, her body hosting adornments of ferns and fungi,
Says to me, "Do not be confused. The fate of humanity will never be
Determined by masturbating men who find strength in
The suffering of others. Never."
"Look here," my queenly guardian says,
Pointing to where she was burned and scarred and how
In that very place now another tree is growing, with embryonic
Fingers
Reaching towards fanning grasses.
My Tall Mother Tree touches my face then,
Redirecting my gaze to her translucent
Greens that shift from vetiver to emerald,
Chartreuse, to shamrock and then to sage.
"You can dance like this," she says to me,
Remaining absolutely still while the rivers of life flow within her.
"I will show you how."
Her voice is deep, androgynous, and the humming grows louder.
She gestures to her thick carpeted floor

With root pathways to antiquity.

"This is the library of tomorrow," she says.

"Look here, in my verdant belly."

"Here is where there is no interruption in truth."

"There, in this place, your vision will be hydrated, liberated from Distraction."

"Even my sisters who were burned," she says,

"Are whole now and ready to sing."

"Do not be deceived. Putin and his ilk do not shape the future."

"They never have. They never will."

"Look here, in my belly," she continues, pointing again to her core,

"This is where you incubated."

"Here is the truth. Keep your gaze here, in my lushness."

"Share the harvest of your vision with everyone."

Titration

The tears of Afghan women
Are in my pulses now.
The air they breathe in,
Sharp with the sting of shock,
Is in my lungs.
This is a tipping point.
My body goes
Over the edge;
Pushed by betrayal after betrayal.
As warming ocean forms
Swell with urgent messages of drought
And immigrants are thrust out of refuge
By so-called judges,
Titration explodes.
Soma becomes sickened beyond measure
As the tide turns
Inescapably
Towards disease;
Decline.
And then this too reaches a
Tipping point
In the folding, unfolding rhythm that is
Birth.

Outrage confronts

Despair,

And a hand breaks through the

Shattered, cracked field

Like a human

Bloom:

Defiance,

Declaring

We rise,

We rise,

We rise.

I Am the Crone of Endless Tears

I am the Crone of Endless Tears
I walk across fields of war, devastation and violence,
Gathering the spirits of the dead.
In my heart pouch I collect the spirits of children
Sacrificed by the ignorance of man.
I carry their spirits inside the warmth of my garments,
Close to the reverberations of my resonant heartbeat,
So that they contact my silky, rose scented breasts.
I am the Crone of Endless Tears.
I am free of guilt and shame.
I am the grief of transfiguration.
My tears are amniotic fluid,
Balm for tortured spirits who have borne witness to
The failures of humanity.
I alchemize disaster into something so new that it cannot be named.
Some call it The Impossible.
I am the waterway to the distant land of
Hope Resurrected in the Laughter of Children.
I am the Mother's Servant.
I am her River of Anguish.
I am her Outlet of Despair.
I am never far from her love,
Without which I would become
Suffocating sewage.
Mother's love is my buoy,

The love that is beyond forgiveness,
The love that is on the other side of
Sacrifice.
All that is sacrificed passes through my sieve,
The filtering mesh of my
Amniotic tears, strung on a chain that forms
The byway to the new humanity.
My tears overflow and pool.
The landscape ahead upwells to bring forth waterfalls.
Drawn by the soundscape,
I, the Crone of Endless Tears, even when I thought I could go no further,
Take another step.
I see reflected in the pools of despair
The face of the Mother.
And then many other faces appear.
The faces of an eternity of loss.
With my babies close to my heart,
And the spirits of the dead in my cape,
I take yet another step.
I gather up the faceless ones,
Those who have been butchered beyond recognition,
And I look again into the pools of despair and see that
We have a destiny.
A destiny of Resurrection.
A destiny that arises out of blood and rape and torture and
Brutality.
A destiny that arises out of the ravages of inhumanity.
A destiny that is blameless.
A destiny of spaciousness.
A staunch destiny of will and faith.

A destiny of focus.

And even though these horrors seem unfathomable,

I suddenly know that they have been witnessed before,

And that the pools of despair always appear

With the reflection of the Mother.

And I know that I, the Crone of Endless Tears,

I am not merely the transporter of the spirits,

The haven of the betrayed children.

I see that I too have a destiny to be fulfilled by my labors.

A destiny of love.

THE ELEMENTS

I learned about the Five Elements as I became a student of energy medicine and subtle healing. This Taoist teaching matched perfectly, like a missing puzzle piece, with my investigations into neuroscience and neuropsychology. While I knew that this fusion was unparalleled and would likely be criticized by my peers, I could not turn from it.

Now, the Elements are also the prism through which I see the world, my relationships, and what is occurring in the environment. What some might call a disparate assembly of mismatched areas of focus are, instead, a unified field of consciousness. As well, I sense that there is an ancient wisdom coming through this fusion that I am creating. That wisdom is revealed through me, if I have the patience and the fortitude to wait for its fruition. Surprisingly, I think I do.

The Elements I am speaking of are Earth, Water, Wood, Air/Metal, Fire, and a subset of the Fire Element called Primordial Fire. These were first introduced to me by my teacher, Mary Iino Burmeister. Prior to that, I had never heard of them. As I have studied further, the unique representation conveyed by Mary leads to a specific understanding of the Elements that from a developmental perspective is, to my awareness, unavailable elsewhere.

I understood the Elements initially as a way to categorize health phenomena and what Mary called "the attitudes," which was her shortcut term for psychology. As I deepened my investigations, however, the Five Elements expanded into a way of seeing everything.

My studies merged into direct experiences of becoming the Five Elements and somatically participating in their healing dance.

Sensing people and the natural world through the lens of the Five Elements allows me to organize my perceptions and offer unique approaches to healing. The Five Elements have become a life language. They sort my thinking and my services to others. They also refine and filter my personal sensory processes. This may be their greatest gift.

The Five Elements are organic categories in which to place the inundations of perception that are familiar to the wounded healer. They provide order for the poet's neurodiversity and spaciousness for the healer-artist who is part shaman, part clinician. They are, I posit, a key to preventing burnout, secondary traumatization, and compassion fatigue.

Earth Element Rendezvous

The veils are getting thinner
I said to the River.
Her huge flat breasts
Sighed, and sagged even more
As they rested
On her fluid body
That feeds so many.
No one is here with me
In this dense forest,
Humming
Riparian,
Thick with the fur of life.
And I am relieved to be alone,
To feed on the chlorophyll I suckle
Secretly
When I am here with
Her.
Sshh. This is my
Earth Element Rendezvous
At the time of the year
When I will be
Reborn.

The Wood Element Speaks

Sometimes, Wood says,
It is better to hide
In a gully
Where the brook is unseen
And my roots suck the moisture
For a quiet life of waiting.
When all is drawn down
My tendrils,
Dripping with ancient mud,
Will shelter the future.
My belly is like a lava cave
Turned away from the light
Like dark ears
Listening to the wind.
When warm is cold,
And cold is hot;
When light is pain
And shadows offer hope;
When angels flee
And ghosts return, then
This gully will be a springboard
And my wet undergrowth will be food.
The families of Wood are beyond landscape.
We are the unheard storytellers who prefer silence.
We have no memories.

For us, everything is eternal.
Do not doubt that we are form
And formlessness.
When you look at us you only see
A small portion of the Truth.
Just wait until you have learned
To listen differently.
There is no practice or study or book
For this guidance.
Go Dance
Or, in our language,
Gui Dance,
As we do
In the dead of night
If you want to be
A guiding light.

The Art of Differentiation: For the Air Element

Still there is Autumn:
Raucous differentiation
In the season of the Lungs;
Respiration being
The bellows of relationship, and
The savant of discernment.
I call this The Season of Differentiation,
When we tremble to let go.
Quick cello bow strokes of silence
Echo in the forest.
Soft Autumn morning breeze is
Her exhalation
As in orgasmic release that
Casts off
The violence of the world
In triumph
By choice.

Sequoia: Wood Element Keening

High above the
Suicidal San Joaquin Valley
Awash in the dry exhaust of consumption,
Stand mighty henna-toned matriarchs whose
Spreading root structures are silently dying of thirst.
Thousands of years old
These still glamorous guardians of eternity
Are saying farewell to our Mother Earth as
Visitors from below,
Juggling pocket-knives and take-out cups,
Carve their initials into tannin-rich bodies.
Mentors in the art of regeneration,
Having thrived after fire and mutilation,
The Sequoia have begun to succumb.
Even as we pose alongside them and
Stare up at their mighty crowns
As if they were creatures in a side-show,
Exhibits for our entertainment,
They are slipping away,
Reducing their numbers
For the first time in millennia.
Irreversible losses
Strip the tears from behind my eyes,
Reduce me to an outcast,

One who falls to her knees,
Helpless, broken,
Staring in disbelief
At those around me,
Innocent children being led by
The overfed hungry
Who do not see or hear me,
Begging them to stop.

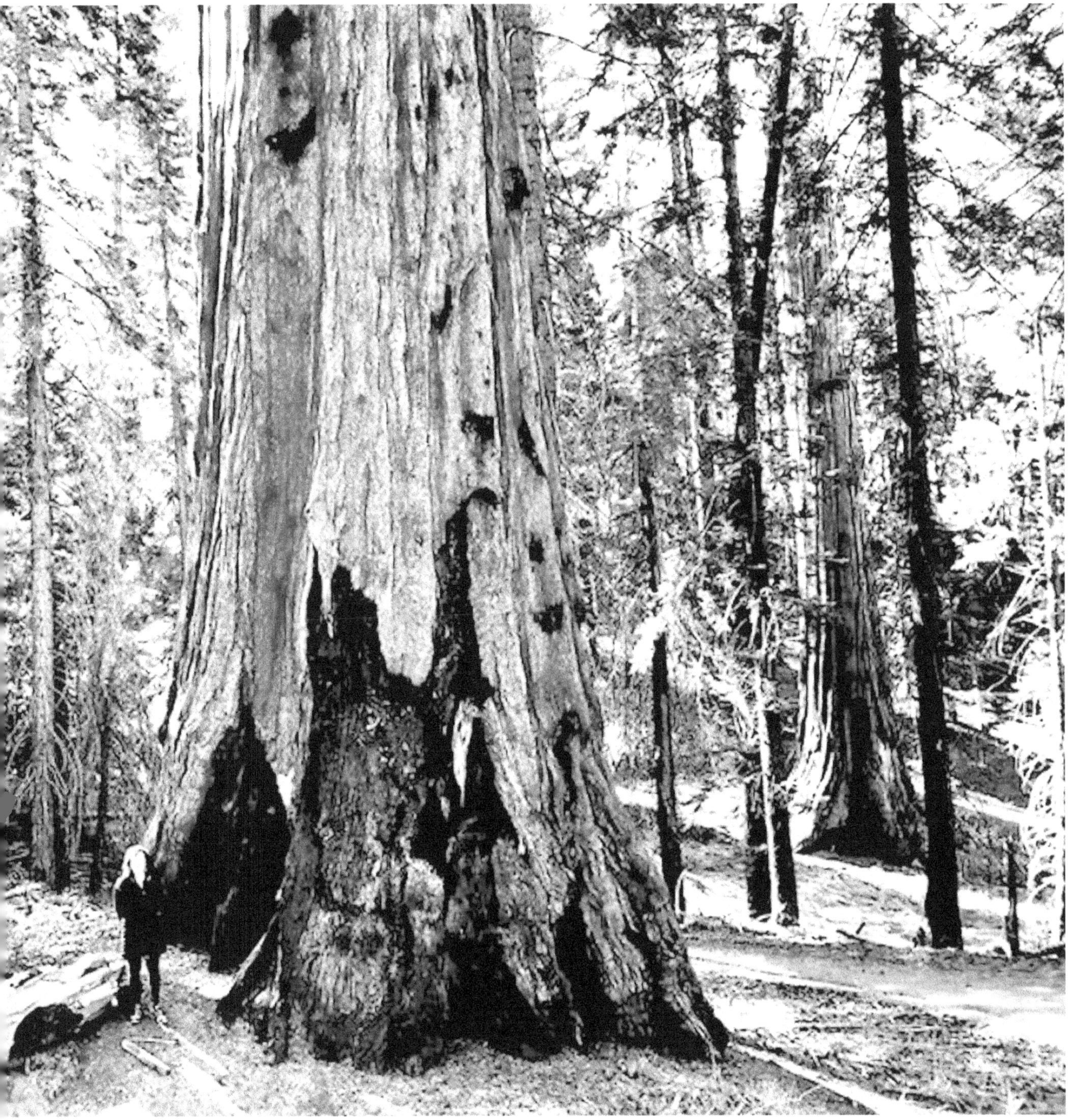

Glare: Glacial Melt

A shield of glare
From the river below
Marks the time,
Frozen and accelerated,
Like glacial debris
Racing towards a meadow,
Slipping from the spooning embrace
Of a coulee
Just as we
Appear to stand still
In our race
To extinction.

Making Fire from Bone

The root systems of our undeniable unity
Are my footpaths in the forest.
My stability demands I pay attention to them.
The soles of my feet strike the strands of an endless web,
Making fire from bone,
Building an eternal alchemical flame.
Let the ash turn to gold now, Mother,
For we are at the end of time.
Let the ash turn to gold,
Shining with our universal brilliance
From a cauldron of new beginnings.
Let the ash turn to gold now, Mother,
For the children of the future.
Give us your voice in all its dialects
So that we speak to everyone and clearly
For you.

I Was Born as Creative Fire

I am giddy with the adornment of words.
Like a magician's mirror they disappear my sagging body,
And make me seductive, tantalizing,
As I was before, without knowing it.
Perhaps that made me more appealing
To predator males seeking to fulfill their wounded feminine.
Now I am emboldened by my wardrobe of words.
I display them wantonly.
They are my countenance, my breasts, my shape,
My everything.
These words mask nothing.
They are neither allure nor pretense.
They are the one beauty I always wanted.
They are all I ever longed for, the true expression of
The eternal soul that I am.
They are the drapery of she who incarnated repeatedly
With one desire: to speak, to form words that match her heart,
To tell the perfect stories that envelop listeners
In loving tales that evolve the mind and draw
Spirits back home
To beauty.

HEALING

I first experienced holistic healing by writing poetry. I had no idea how it happened. How did I even know how to compose poems? No one taught me. Nevertheless, I began and underwent physiological shifts before I even knew what that meant. My capacity to survive, to function, and ultimately to thrive under extremely difficult circumstances evolved, almost with every word I wrote.

It was easy to become addicted to writing. It was, and remains, my drug of choice. I later combined it with movement and energy medicine to make the perfect healing cocktail. This is how I came to know, without anyone's instruction, that I was not the trauma and shock around me.

I don't think the talking style of therapy works well for wounded healers and artists. We might pretend sometimes that it is working because we want so badly to fit in. But all the while we know, in our hearts, that until there is a physiological evolution that manifests in our authentic, cellular core, and remains sustainable, nothing has really happened.

Energy medicine uncovered my true energetic state, which I am still exploring. As many of the poems in this collection indicate, I have been alchemizing the trauma of my life assiduously for some time. Energy medicine was what made the gold possible. The credit goes not only to the system I employed but to my own nervous system and its generosity in responding. This kind of biochemistry is essential for the metallurgy of suffering.

I have also devoted myself to understanding the healing process and particularly the resolution of shock and trauma. We are living in times that will only become increasingly more traumatizing and shocking. My work convinces me that we are destined to go beyond trauma. We are destined to break through to wholeness, to our kinship with our living earth. When that bond is sealed, we will know what to do, and we will just do it. That is healing.

Regenerative Health for a Climate Changing World is the paradigm I developed as a byproduct of this understanding of true healing. It speaks to my fusion of poetry and science, activism and motherhood, health justice advocate and healthcare provider. The Regenerative Health paradigm is the bridge I have built between personal healing, social responsibility, and activism. In order to do anything at all for others I had to devote myself to healing. Originally built for self-healing, the Regenerative Health paradigm elicits such enthusiasm and compassion that it has to be shared.

The Great Physician

The Great Physician
Is she who knows
The metallurgy of grief.
She transmutes vilification,
Betrayal,
Scapegoating,
Gaslighting,
Torture,
Finger-pointing,
Blaming,
Castigation,
And all manner of ignorance
Into enthusiasm for the future of humanity.
As truth rises to the surface of my body.
Bones mend, tendons re-knit,
Joints ease and
Resilience arises.
Heart feeds mind poems,
Healthcare strategies and
The architecture of leadership.
The Great Physician breathes the
Recipe for making poison into medicine.
This is the Destiny of Fulfillment.

Who Are You?

You are the one who
Folded and Unfolded
In rhythmic undulations
Perfectly timed
To orchestrate your dance of being.
You are the one who
Differentiated your cells
Separating and reforming
Ectoderm
Mesoderm
Endoderm.
You are the Director of Organogenesis.
You are the Initiator,
The one who understands everything
And therefore, forgives everything.
You wield the Sword of Apoptosis,
Remorselessly transitioning, discarding, evolving.
You are the Compass of the Sacred Directions
Dorsal
Ventral
Cranial
Caudal.
You are the Germinator,
The One who Begins the Great Migrations:
The Ingression through the Primitive Streak,

The Voyage through the Womb.

You enticed your mother to build a placenta for you,

To surrender all her gateways,

And she complied.

You are the One who Does Not Wait.

Because you know,

You act.

American Waiting Room

The round-faced woman turns to me and says,
"My baby sister is dying. I'm saving up for a
Hot air balloon ride. It's on her bucket list.
There is nothing they can do about it."
My hand goes to my heart.
"You are a wonderful sister," I say.
The woman pulls out her phone and
Shows me a photo of her sister
Pouring a vodka martini into her feeding tube.
"I'm retired now," she continues.
Then she points to her red, swollen ankle, and says,
"I had surgery there but since then I can barely walk."
On the other side of the room a
Mom is shushing her agitated son who
Keeps hitting his head with his clenched fist.
Mom adjusts her body to hide her child,
Glancing furtively towards the others in the room.
The receptionist returns to her computer screen.
Her long fingernails are painted green with shamrocks
For St. Patrick's Day
They click rhythmically as she types.
The scent of a microwave meal
Wafts through the cold air.
Scenes of a bombed-out Ukrainian city
Flash on the silenced television screen above us, and

Then transitions to a
Newscaster, immaculate and perfectly attired, seated
Behind an s-shaped acrylic desk
In a room that rotates as if on a turntable of tragedies.
I find my neutrality in the room I share with humanity.
I identify the midline of my being,
Awash with grief and rage, grief and rage, grief and rage.
In my silence I unite with everyone:
The round-faced woman, her sister, the mom, the receptionist,
But especially the boy obscured by his mother's body.
His muffled, uncontrollable sounds
Renew my commitment to my destiny.

The Black Madonna

Mother of the lost tribe
Madonna of the magnetic earth
Madonna exuding the nectar of spiritual sensuality
Ecstasy of God's merger with the Feminine Divine
Madonna of the lonely wanderer
Madonna of the empty handed
Madonna of the abandoned child
Madonna of the blood shed by the Christ
Madonna of the sacred wound
Madonna of my broken heart
Madonna in the palms of my pleading hands
Madonna of my father's sin
Madonna of the world of darkness
Madonna of the mystery
Madonna of the unspoken
Mother who guards the amber box scented with myrrh
Mother who holds in her heart the innocence at the core of all People
Mother who sees our oneness
Mother who is our shelter
Mother of the temple of the dark truth
Mother who grants us freedom,
Her child blooming from her breast.

Beyond Traumatic Repetition

A shadow hangs over the world.
It seeps into my bones.
It twists my structure until
I am bent in prayer, a supplicant.
What more can I do to uplift this burden?
Whether innovator, migrant, outlaw or rogue.
Whether scientist, artist, mystic or visionary,
Whether mother, grandmother, sister or daughter,
Whether wife, colleague, ally or enemy,
In whatever form I take, I differentiate.
I shake off the curse of traumatic repetition.
Every poem, paradigm, protocol and theory,
Every book, essay, response and testament,
Is a ceremony of redemption.
I shake off the curse of traumatic repetition.
It is over. It is over. It is over.
The bridge has been built between all the worlds.
We are one.

Trauma, You Have Schooled Me

Trauma, my beloved,
You have schooled me.
You have taught me to write poems
To the mute rhythmic music of my isolation,
On the blank slates of my escapades,
Those countless encounters with death
That no one knows anything about until I
Draw them up from the well of my
Haunted memory.
Trauma, I have been dragged on your twisted path
Like a slave in chains, and now
I have harnessed you and now
I ride you,
Wild stallion of my irrefutable history.
Trauma: You have my
Middle name, the name of Russia,
The dark forest of the Elders where
Twisted trees obscure the blood of tortured
Men and women, frozen in the steppes of the
Vain attempt to escape from trauma.
Shock, like an over bright sun:
You are the lamp, the illumination, neon-like,
The stage director, choreographer, conductor,
You integrate a thousand trauma interludes into
an epic,

A story of all women,
Raped and exploited,
Colonized and dominated, the
Epic
I will write before
I die.

The Texture of Oppression

In the bodies of the women who come to me for healing
I feel the texture of oppression:
Strings of coagulated holding back in musculature,
Poison pellets of self-rejection, inserted deeply into connective tissue.
Taut tendons entwine bone like strangulation vines emitting
Venomous inflammation.
I touch the ectoderm of centuries of agony,
The mesoderm of shock, and
The braced membrane of endoderm, defiant and impenetrable.
Fluids meant to flow are backed up, filling
Avenues of expression with sediment, making them
Pathways of refusal.
Latched back doors to the heart long to swing open to the front,
To release the pent-up spontaneity that has been damned.
The time has come, my sisters,
To disbar the court that silences us from within.
The time has come to detoxify the texture of oppression
From our flesh, and
Come out from the eddy of repetitious restraint.

We can do this.
We can irrigate with rivulets of permission,
With waves of validation and recognition, the
Brine of wisdom that is the song, the poem, the art of
The crone. Invoke, supplicate
She who dwells in our wombs, she who knows
How we give birth to ourselves.

THE EVOLUTION OF CONSCIOUSNESS

As I continue to manifest Climate Change & Consciousness, sustain our community and simultaneously develop the healthcare paradigm of Regenerative Health, an evolution in my consciousness occurs. I am redefining both consciousness and healthcare in the context of facing climate crisis. This is not an easy or smooth process. Weaving so much together is a chaotic and wild ride that I embrace, more and more, as my dance forward.

One consistent thread, however, is that I leave my old self behind every day; every hour. The relational challenges, the insistent passion of my commitment, the obstacles that appear—sometimes one after the other with no breathing space—insist that I change the very nature of who I am. Problem-solving is not a methodology to learn. It is a surrender that melts resistance out of necessity. Prayer becomes the only reasonable methodology, because it is clear that nothing else works. I am becoming someone I do not recognize.

This is the uncontrollable evolution of consciousness that accords to those who step into action that flows from a passionate, irrational love for humanity.

> *You have to act as if it were possible to radically transform the world. And you have to do it all the time.*
>
> —Angela Davis

The Line

Endless Mother,
Feminine Origin of All,
Darkness from which we came,
I beg for the mercy we do not deserve,
Having squandered everything.
We have crossed the line, and it is red
With the blood of children,
The mark of our consuming sickness.
I beg the mycorrhizal undertow of wisdom,
The network of fluid innocence,
The purity of life's embryonic intention,
To redeem us from our ignorance.
Reclaim, rediscover, regenerate truth of purpose
In our voices, our actions,
So that we retrieve the lost beauty
We know as health, as alignment, as
Integrity.
Endless Mother,
Feminine Origin of All,
Darkness from which we came,
Stand with us on this red line and
With your wisdom touch
Move us to the curative place
Of Original Brilliance,
The Pure Genius that is the approaching
Groundswell that carries us beyond hope.

The Embryo, Climate Crisis, and the Pandemic

At each stage of its development, whenever it seemed that an impasse had been reached, the most improbable solutions emerged that enabled the Earth to continue its development.
— Thomas Berry

My spunky embryonic self
Encounters this era
As if it were the sacral-coccygeal promontory.
This is the forbidding peninsula every baby
Must navigate before she frees herself of restrictions.
It is the penultimate challenge of
The shaping compression of birth.
Embryo me forges improbable solutions
From the cave of becoming
Where there are no authorities to consult,
Only embryonic radar and an embodied compass.
Alert, focused, tireless, she
Eyes the forbidding bluff defiantly
And draws from the continuity
That is the bottomless indwelling,
The nameless, unpredictable, irrational
Suddenness that sparks movement,
Brilliant movement:
A meaningful risk,
With excruciating consequences
Before the limitless liberation.

My Crone Years

And the fire in my soul burns as if I were just born.
Is it only the beauty of my words that are left for me?
I wear them like bracelets for my healing hands.
My shadow on the forest floor meets me.
She bends down while my spirit ascends.
I defy the manipulation of this decaying culture, but
Of what value are the protests of an old woman who writes poems
Begging people to rise up?
O my dying country,
You sacrifice your brilliance for cheap toys.
Still, I cry, "My God it is you who has delivered me for these times."
So, I will not shut up or shut down.
I am yet the star child brought forth
For some hidden redemption.
In that ropey, tangled under sand of the forest floor
Made by the wanderings of my people,
Down there in the dusty tunnels
With the infinitesimal creatures we depend on, there
Is my salvation, my family that
Cultivates my stubborn, resurgent entelechy.

Raw

Homage to the End and the Beginning

I am raw; unmasked on the precipice to extinction.
The moss-laden, soft gestures of the Mother Trees surrounding me
Beckon me to their breasts to suck the thick colostrum
In the lining of their time tattooed skin.
Soon I will be one of them;
Rooted, with owls and sparrows in my limbs,
Hushed and at rest for once and for all.
There is an unbreakable bond between creativity and activism,
Joy, health, beauty and rage.
With the flowering wounds of sexual abuse guiding
My hands, my voice my mind,
I know that the rape of my body and the rape of the earth are one.
Violation, as in pillage of the innocent,
Was my primal instruction;
Initiation onto the path of
Love for humanity and
Devotion to the unseen.
Behind the madness of extraction is
The broken-hearted distortion of love,
Which is greed.
My words are my redemption.
I stand with the violated as we attune
To the soundscape of tomorrow,
A concert of embryonic musician oracles,
Playing unceasingly for the world we adore.

Grandmother at the End of Time

I am the Grandmother at the End of Time
Who draws a circle of protection for the universal unborn.
My shawl is fringed with the glint of aspen leaves,
The sparkle of elfin-gold luminous moss,
And the iridescence of snakes.
It is the flag at the gateway to the new world.
My wild hair is threaded with future dreams, and
The make-believe refrains of children at play.
My old, bright eyes illuminate the way for migrants
Carrying their little ones on their backs.
My clothes are dyed with sequoia tannin,
Quilted with crushed cottonwood leaves,
And ornamented with owl feathers and fox fur.
I moan in unrecorded languages and
Keen in the secret tongues of the hidden
Whose life shares were stolen by the lonely covetous.
I am the Grandmother at the End of Time
Whose breath is the wind that turns the page
In the last chapter of the Book of Alienation.
I die to a new ancient song,
The best one ever written.
It was memorized centuries ago, and
Encoded in the soles of my feet
That are hardened and tough
From my endless pacing on the
Desertified carpet of our ravaged earth.

Balance

My left foot
Is ankle deep
In the losses of my mother.
The toes sift the ashes
Of migration
At the bottom of that well.
My right foot
Sinks deeper every hour
Into the cold cross currents
Of cruelty and courage
At the confluence of this
Code Red River of blood.
My unique balance
Comes from keeping at bay
Rhetoric and data,
Predictions, curses and omens.
I have been forced into
Focus and Presence
As my only tools of
Evolution from the moment
I was conceived.
I am an ancient nymph,
A scientist of the murky underworld,
A sensory microscope

Enlarging the potential of
Humanity.
I defy the brutal
Weaponry of politics,
That repeatedly stabs
The dreams of the innocent.
Powerless and insistent,
Broken-hearted and unrelenting,
I feed on the contradictions
That accompany my solitude
And crowd my dreams
With the illustrations of Interbeing.

Mother

She shows me her face;
There, where the old growth hemlocks and alder
Tower and crowd closely to one another.
Her cheeks are plump with lanky and beaked moss.
She is full with smiling at the sight of me
Looking back at her.
It seems not so long ago
That I listened alone
To the sighing of the night,
The violence of the streets
And the loud emptiness of
Narrow passageways, and
Sat to meals of frightening food
In the chilling, ceaseless grey.
Now 77 years later I greet her at last,
Author of my cells.
"I am your Mother,"
She says simply.
Her soft voice carries easily across
The cold, rippling belly of her Sandy River
As the gold confetti of the season
Flowers the graveyard of her salmon.
Despite our mourning we are overjoyed to be together,
Just as refugees wearing barbed wire crowns of thorns
Meet at the border crossing.

The dirge at the end of time plays in the mist,
Yet nothing can taint the primordial fire
Ignited by this reunion.
"I am your Mother," she whispers.
Her hot breath dries the blood on our faces
As we melt into one another.
Fatigue evaporates like sweat off a colicky infant.
Though hushed with love, her words are amplified
Through the vaporous megaphone of my body.
I join her in the fog draped hillsides of spikerush and hydrilla,
Willow and rushes, and in the
Dense, ropey underbrush of pathways glutted with mulching oak
Leaves.
The moisture oozes through my tissue
As she teaches me to melt into this immersion in trust.
"I am your Mother," she repeats,
"And this is the way to fight;
This is the way of action,
This is the way to meet the ignorance of others who do not see me,
Who do not know that I am their Mother."
My eyes are closed and when I open them
I look again into the old growth canopy,
Into what once was the mundane vista just on the other side of the
River,
Out my kitchen window,
Where I stand to wash the dishes.

After

There will be a reunion.
We will recognize each other
And embrace warmly,
Relieved for the future of our children
And all the unborn of this earth.
The hard work,
The unmeasurable grief and loss
Will be honored by everyone.
There will be no separation,
No name calling,
No hierarchy,
No forms to complete
Or tests to pass;
No exclusion
Or penalties;
No pre-requisites
Or book-keeping.
It will be spacious then with
Room for the Elders to rest
Comfortably,
And the little ones will make them laugh
Easily.
The time of fragmentation
Will be enshrined
As our wisdom teaching,

Integrated into our flesh

Like stigmata,

Tattoos of horrific

Hubris

That we can never repeat

Having learned from the Great Mercy

How to distinguish

Lies from

Truth.

The Earth Inhabits My Mind

The Earth inhabits my mind
Like a lover I am about to lose.
I pursue her, desperate
For reassurance;
One last touch of connection,
Warm with recognition of our eternal bond.
But she is slipping from me;
Her bright coral blush whitening,
No longer pulsating with the blood of seduction;
Her verdant chlorophyll is
Browning at the tips of her exquisite limbs
That once gathered me into her.
She looks tired of my presence.
I have betrayed her too any times
And our destiny is on the rocks.
The Earth inhabits my mind,
And I panic.
The truth is:
I may have already lost her.

THE HUMAN FAMILY

One of the most surprising and glorious transformations that has emerged on this path of the wounded healer is my felt sense of belonging in the human family.

I grew up believing that I, and my immediate family members, were outcasts. We pretended to act as if we belonged. There was constant shame because of this, the kind of shame from which there is no relief. We were always hiding our truth, our shame, our language, our origins, our poverty, our fear, and our desperation to belong. This desperation was linked inextricably with the fear of annihilation. We had always been threatened with annihilation. It followed us everywhere.

In the reclamation of my voice and my right to be just as I am, I knew somatically, cellularly, that I not only deserved to be seen and heard, but that I carried a piece of the human puzzle. I still need to reassure myself of this and counteract the criticism that this is hubris.

The poems in this collection reflect the readiness—that increases daily—to share my unique perceptions with my larger human family.

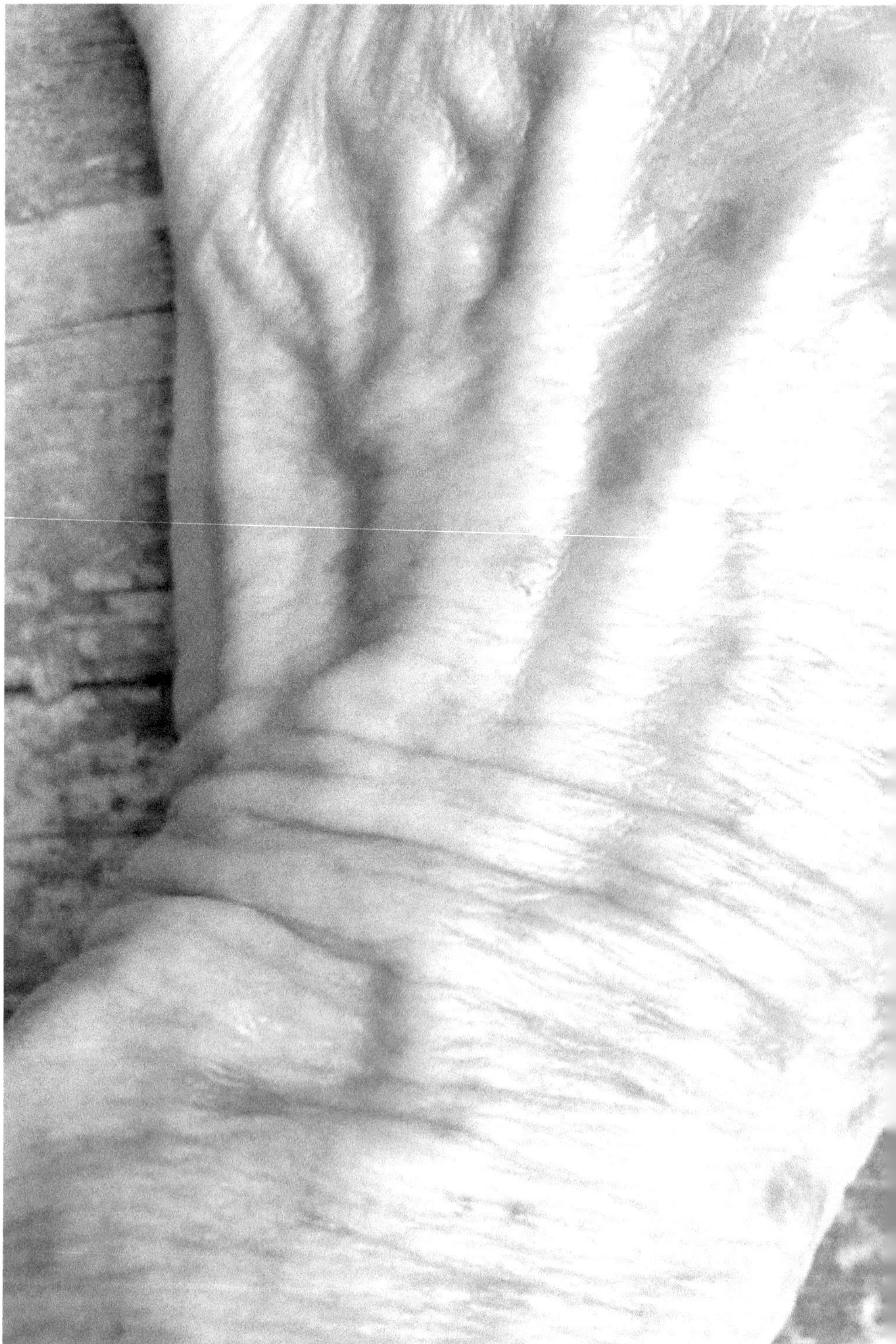

Eldering

This is not aging. These are the ropes of antiquity like the tree roots that are my ground in the forest home where I commune with my mothers. This is not aging. It is maturing into my true self at last. These ropey strands are my path, finally emerging from all the hard work, the deep dreaming, the prescient secrets harbored in my soul. The map is now my appendage, magnetized to our living earth; instrument of my heart.

Raw #2

Have you had enough loss yet, I ask myself.
Are you tired of burying your grief in spiritual bypass
And false optimism?
The lies I told myself
Like an addict,
The rescuer I have always been
Who wants to fix the mess, and
Cover it with silk and smiles, are rotting.
And now I must grieve.
Grieve with gritty, ravaged, buried faith;
Grieve with the rage of a colonized slave;
Grieve with the raspy voice of my
Animal love and devotion;
All that has been suffocated and stuffed
Until I am almost a zombie.
Almost.
But not yet.
"Not quite yet,"
The Merlin bird told me.
"Not quite yet,"
The Sanderlings said,
As they raced their silver wings
In the back and forth, back and forth,
Of their collective divining;
An orchestra of feather winds.

Not quite yet

Said the Loon, and the Tern,

And the Cedar Waxwing,

And the Cormorant,

While I wept and roared

And begged for their forgiveness.

Broadcast from a Nation in Mourning

Tutored by survivors of genocide,
I recognize the signals.
Genocide of children is suicide spelled differently.
It is the headline here in the United States of America.
Words arrive twisted from the mouths of those who claim to
Speak for us.
How dare they?
Do we empower them?
Only the voiceless require a spokesperson,
And marionettes, painted dolls manipulated by others.
One woman's voice,
One grandmother's voice,
One defiant voice,
Added to another,
And another,
And another.
Will our fingers pick up the bloodied thread of
The weave that unites us?
Can our voices come from an ageless source that lives within us?
Can we interweave ourselves with all the
Unrelenting voices that together clear a pathway through the
Lies?

One woman's voice,
One grandmother's voice,
One defiant voice,
Added to another,
And another,
And another.

No Waiting

Waiting to be seen as valuable
Is like waiting for a politician to become authentic.
It's like waiting for a salesperson promoting spritiual programming
To tell the truth.
It's like a survivor of domestic violence
Waiting for the perpetrator to stop beating her.
When you are done, really done, with waiting,
You look into your own eyes in the mirror
Long enough for them to look back at you
And transmit the irrefutable realization of your
Giftedness, so that it is imprinted forever.
And then you see the women around you
Who are waiting to be seen,
And you know how to speak to them
So that they stop waiting
And become their destiny of
Leadership and it is easy
So much easier than anyone imagined.
It is as easy as feeling the winds of time.
It is as easy as smiling at a child.
It is as easy as honoring your legacy.
It is as easy as a flower opening,
As water moving toward its source,
As birds singing to one another,
Above the din of the streets.

Creativity Rising

This [Creativity Rising] is not a poem.
It is the articulation of the antennae
Of my being.
It is output from the
Unified field of consciousness that is
Dancing with generational and generative
Forces of transmutation.
Etheric artists from the realms of Pure Action
Nurture us into the
Beauty we are born to embody.
They shine into our minds
The brilliant world that
Our children deserve to inhabit.
They activate the universal kindness that
Forgives and redeems us.
Creativity Rising is not a poem.
It is a manifesto of vital intention that is
Rooted in the mycorrhizal underworld
Of substance, soil, fungi, ferment, and microbes.
Creativity Rising is not a poem.
It is the unpredictable descent of wisdom.
It is the mystery of surrender to the presences
That invite us, when we are aligned by prayer or desperation,
To allow the erasure of foolish logic,
The crumbling of all conclusions.

Creativity Rising is not a poem.
It is the wingspan of destiny.

TRUE EMBODIMENT

True embodiment is revolutionary. It is anti-colonial, non-extractive, anti-capitalist and non-dualistic. It cannot be sold, purchased, promoted, marketed or certified. It rises up from the soles of feet that are rooted in the dirt. It is an anti-inflammatory medicine. True embodiment is ready to heal you right now and launch you into decisive action for our living Mother Earth.

Before I Die

For All Climate Refugees

Before I die

My words will

Live in my cells

Like my DNA.

My legs will walk my poems.

The words of my truth

Will be wings

That move my body

Wherever it is called from within.

And I will go

Fearlessly, effortlessly,

Like a bird guided only

By its interior compass.

I will fly where I must

To gather

The lost tribes

Of the Children of Light,

All those who have seen

Their legs torn from under them,

All those who have been

Ripped from their homes.

All these people,

Like me,

Are the Messiahs of the Future,
And we will fly together
As one flock,
Going home.

The Distance of the Night
For the Suicides

Who can measure the distance of the night
Or the velocity of its movements
That roils the blood of the disturbed?
Night oozes like black tar
Slowly spreading through loneliness.
My friends have slipped
Under this dark water of night,
Men with eyes of fire
And impossible tenderness.
I reach for them now
Though they have fallen
Before this moment.
I reach across the dimensions
And pull them to me
Fearlessly,
Holding nothing back,
Pulling them to me,
Feeling their tears seep into my flesh.
The beads of their longing
Penetrate me,
Making me bleed
Willingly.
I will never say good-bye.
I make a vow

To hunt down the killer,
The madness that said
They were worthless,
The insecurity that took their
Breath.
I will hunt down that killer
With every word I say
Until their beauty
Rises again
And their eyes shine
And they tell us
What happened to them,
And what they know,
And what they learned
In the distance of the night.

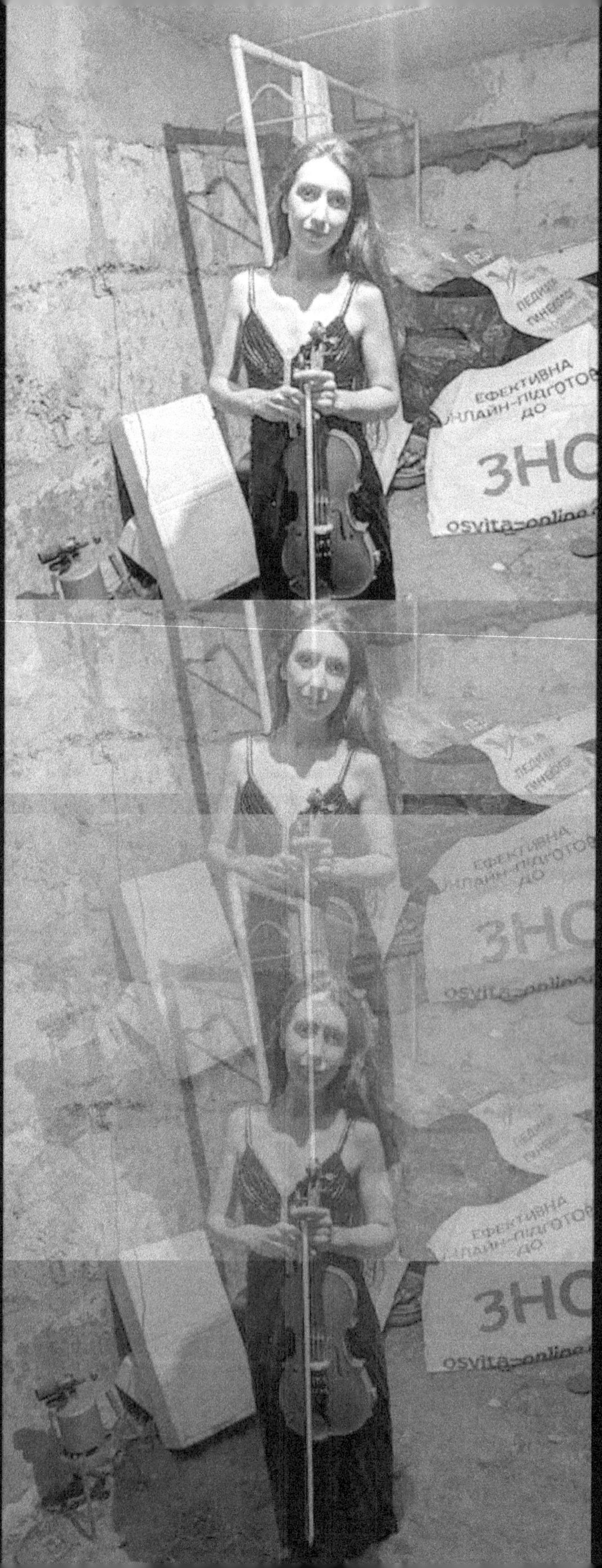

I Am the Violinist in the Bomb Shelter

I rise with the rush of love in my fingertips,
Each digit insistent, grasping to touch the world.
My eyes are draped with aching to see renewal,
The springtime of humanity,
The stunned re-membering of the truth:
The realization of unity.
Just as I longed for my mother and father to stop killing each other,
Just as I waited and waited for them to say,
"We forgot about you, precious vulnerable beings, please forgive us.
Let us repair the world together, as our faith decrees,"
So do I long for this awakening.
I rise with the rush of love in my fingertips.
The motion of reaching is so familiar.
I think of the violinist in the bomb shelter,
Or the cellist playing in the rubble of his homeland,
Or the child in the refugee camp standing to sing
And everyone becomes silent, recalling original brilliance.
I am the violinist in the bomb shelter
Who continues to play whether or not anyone listens.
I am she who has become
The violin of the Mother, delivering a sonata of her
Longing to reunite with her children
And feel them close to her again.

We Are the Messenger Birds

Every day I give thanks for the shelter of these cedars
With their slender ebony trunks
Stretching ecstatically to Sky Father.
The delicate fingers of my ancient guardians
Playfully stroke the ethereal mist
Between realms
While I marvel at the beauty.
Messenger birds live in these shelters;
Never homeless.
There are perches aplenty
For resting and eating,
And feeding the young,
For singing and sharing stories
Until the rocking cradles
Are rattled and shaken by the wind.
Then the messenger birds fly off.
Their vision scrolls are wound around
Stalk legs and sealed with gold.
Are we not the messenger birds?
Are we not poised between dimensions,
Shaken from our comfort and thrust into
Ambiguity; forced to fly
With our assignments hidden somewhere
In our bodies?

Can we stop long enough now
And read the script
We wrote ourselves,
The code we created,
And deciphered,
That can now be
Delivered?

In the Time of Massacres, My Grandmothers Awaken Me

My grandmothers
Sophie and Shoshana.
One the wife of the shochet,
The other the wife of a shreyder
Who tried to run a candy store in the Bronx,
And failed.
One Sephardic,
The other Ashkenazi.
They turned their backs on each other.
Now they stand before me,
Their arms entwined,
Looking like sisters.
I rub my eyes.
Sophie has lost her haunted sadness,
The brooding darkness that hung about her
Like a shroud.
And Shoshana, who was wild eyed and desperate,
Harangued by poverty and too many mouths to feed,
Is serene, soft, loving.
I never knew them like this.
They come to me before dawn
When I am davening for the massacred children,
All of them,
The children of Israel, the children of Gaza.
They come to me when I am davening
For the precious innocents
Caught in the ravenous cycles of revenge.

They recognize me now.
"We are sorry," they say.
"We could not see you before."
"There was a film over our eyes,"
It was the film of war; it was the haze
Of brutality inflicted on our people.
"It blinded us. We are sorry."
They step forward and they each place one hand on my head.
"Shenalach," they say, almost whispering,
"Momelah," the terms of endearment so rare to my ears,
"We give you the power of peace."
"We give you the untapped resilience of generations."
"We give you the voice of leadership."
"We impart to you the links of unification,
Never before used but awaiting this moment."
Suddenly there is a bottom in the well of my
Tears of uselessness and impotence,
The tears of helpless victimization and
Smallness in the face of what appears to be
The power of destruction,
There is a bottom to that well and that
Bottom is the platform from which I spring
Into the heart of compassion that is
My destiny.
And I am whole.
I am a force to be reckoned with.
I am many armed and
Visionary, and
I am the latent spirit
Of my two grandmothers

And the long line of

Peacemakers I never knew before,

Who now step forward,

Women of valor.

The curtain of the hidden world is parted

By my two grandmothers,

Sophie and Shoshana.

Their unification unifies everything

Behind me and before me.

The vision of peace is possible.

Indeed, it is done.

I continue davening for the massacred children,

The children of Gaza and the children of Israel,

All of our massacred children,

Each moving out of horror to the liberating light

Of the oneness we know.

Glossary

Shochet: Kosher butcher
Shreyder: Tailor
Shenalach: Pretty One
Momelah: Dear One
Davening: Praying with a swaying motion

THE GREAT TURNING

It was on that fateful night in November 2016 that the Great Turning moved like a cyclone through my body. Everything changed in an instant. Just as I collapsed into despair and incredulity at the election of someone who had no right to occupy the People's House, so did I, simultaneously, rise up. I rose, in the same instant, with a vision, a mission, a direction that I could not, from that moment forward, abandon. There was the feeling of being possessed, chosen. In a radically different way from what I was witnessing on the television screen, I was elected.

My priorities rearranged themselves. The blueprint of my life was redrawn. I became a climate activist. Not the kind who marches and carries a sign. Rather I was instructed to arouse the climate activist in every human being and raise a chorus of voices for our living earth. I had no idea why I was told to create Climate Change & Consciousness as a global community. I had never done anything like that before. But it was not possible for me to question this directive. This was my Great Turning.

Initially, there was the assignment of creating a major conference to awaken awareness. I intuitively knew where it was to be and who should be there. Climate Change & Consciousness was born from this conference, which I convened in 2019 in Scotland. Four hundred people attended on-site and as many attended on-line. Bill McKibben, Christiana Figueres, Vandana Shiva, Uncle Angaangaq, Charles Eisenstein and Xiuhtezcatl Martinez were some of the stunning speakers rousing us, young and old alike, to wake up. This was just the beginning. Since then, this community has continued, despite pandemic and war, to embody the mystery and, yes, the promise of the Great Turning.

It was the revered Joanna Macy who employed the term the Great Turning to mark humanity's existential crisis. With straightforward elegance she opened us to our grief at extinction. With her Bodhisattva mind, Joanna Macy created the spaciousness we needed to match our inner experience to the outer catastrophe that was accelerating before our eyes. Joanna Macy taught us to hold hopelessness and active hope in the same body and to never give up. I do this now every day. Poetry helps to make this possible.

If this volume succeeds in the relay for humanity to pass the torch, then I am fulfilled.

About the Author

Dr. Stephanie Mines is the author of more than a dozen books that reflect her three decades of research as a neuroscientist and embryologist. She has investigated shock and trauma as a survivor, a professional, a clinical researcher, and a healthcare provider. Her work has resulted in her nonprofit, The TARA Approach, which provides practical means for the systemic change she promotes as a Regenerative Health paradigm. Her training and healing modalities are used by individuals internationally and by professional counselors and organizations such as addiction clinics, abuse centers, and refugee charities.

In her autobiographical poetry and prose, Dr. Mines shares how her personal and professional background shaped her insights into a fusion of trauma recovery and climate activism. In her global activism through her Climate Change & Consciousness nonprofit, Dr. Mines focuses on humanity's forward moving direction where inner and outer climates meet. In that place of mystery is our connection with the natural world and the living systems waiting to communicate with us, to give us what data cannot record.

In 2019, Dr. Mines convened a global conference in Scotland with 400 in-person attendees and an equal number attending via media. In 2023, she opened the first Regenerative Health graduate school program through Ubiquity University. The graduate program integrates Dr. Mines' trauma recovery and climate activism strategies for individual and planetary healing.

The Great Physician: Medicinal Poetry for the Anthropocene is Dr. Mines' first major collection of poems. Poetry, she says, helps make possible "the spaciousness needed to match our inner experience to the outer catastrophe that is accelerating before our eyes. It helps us to understand." These poems are inner experiences through which she, and indirectly the reader, find a way to understand planetary experience, personal and generational cause and effect, and hopefully, the courage and energy to change organically—from war, intolerance, fear, ennui.

As an acclaimed poet, Dr. Mines is the winner of the Joseph Henry Jackson Award for Poetry for her series The Nocturnes. She also received grants from the National Endowment for the Arts for her work developing poetry workshops in communities that resulted in several chapbooks of community poetry. As a founding member of the Poetry in Schools Program, she taught within the program for almost a decade in California and Colorado.

In addition to *The Great Physician: Medicinal Poetry for the Anthropocene*, Dr. Mines' books include the acclaimed works—*The Secret of Resilience: Healing Personal and Planetary Trauma Through Morphogenesis*, (2023) and *We Are All In Shock: Energy Healing for Traumatic Times*, (2020).

You can follow Stephanie's work on her website at www.StephanieMines.com. You can also read her ongoing Crone Speak blog series on her website and on her Substack account at https://substack.com/@stephaniemines.

Praise for the Work of Dr. Stephanie Mines

The ideas of the TARA Approach are accessible. The biochemistry is relevant, authoritative, up-to-date, and presented as a fascinating account of nature's handiwork. The techniques are easily applied and are effective.

—**Donna Eden**, Author of *Energy Medicine*

In a world of constant debilitating shock, Stephanie Mines offers skillful means to resolve personal and collective wounding in ways that illuminate as well as heal.

—**Jean Houston, PhD**, Author of *A Mythic Life: Learning to Live Our Greater Story*

Stephanie Mines focuses on giving people simple and effective tools that they can preventatively use in a multitude of potentially traumatic situations.

—**Peter Levine, PhD**, Founder of Somatic Experiencing
Author of *Waking the Tiger, Healing Trauma*, and *Trauma Proofing Your Kids*

Dr. Mines evolves the pioneering work of one of her early mentors, Dr. Peter Levine, and provides a needed component in the treatment of trauma.

—**William Emerson, PhD**, Author of *Shock, A Universal Malady*

Stephanie Mines, moves through the complex territory of healing with refreshing grace, candor and immense wisdom.

—**Pat Ogden, PhD**, Founder of Sensorimotor Psychotherapy Institute
Author of *Trauma and the Body*

This work you are offering is validating the human experience in a way that all of my schooling and all of therapy did not touch.

—**Sheila Norquay**

Dr. Stephanie Mines has dedicated her life to a brilliant exploration of embryology. In that exploration she has found the secret to resilience that is the key to meeting these chaotic and heartbreaking times.

—**Dr. Clare Willocks, MD, OBGYN**, Founder of Bridging the Healthcare Gap

Dr. Stephanie Mines reveals that it is possible for every one of us to heal, and that we can be trauma-preventative moving forward. Her Regenerative Health paradigm demonstrates that we can heal the children of our time, contribute to the healing of our planet, and in the process, ensure the health and well-being of each other and our collective future.

—**Mary Spalding, MFA**, Waldorf Educator

Milton Keynes UK
Ingram Content Group UK Ltd.
UKHW021432190624
444161UK00002B/7

9 781736 651711